M000033422

I CARRY YOUR

Heart

IN MINE

Creating a Meaningful Life after the Death of a Spouse

◇◇◇◇◇◇◇◇◇◇◇◇◇◇◇◇◇◇◇◇◇◇◇◇◇◇

JOHN F. ROSKOPF

JILL SCHOENEMAN-PARKER, PSY. D.

I Carry Your Heart in Mine: *Creating a Meaningful Life after the Death of a Spouse*

By John F. Roskopf with contributing author Jill Schoeneman-Parker

ABOUT THE AUTHORS

John F. Roskopf retired after a 45-year career in finance and risk management, most recently focusing on risk management issues in higher education. He has spoken frequently on organizational strategy, leadership and creativity and has published numerous articles on risk management. John received a B.S. from Quincy University and an M.B.A. from Loyola University. He is the father of two and grandfather of four.

Jill Schoeneman-Parker, Psy. D. received her doctorate from the Illinois School of Professional Psychology with a specialization in Abuse and Trauma. Additionally, she trained in art therapy at George Washington University following her studies at Wellesley College. She is a Licensed Clinical Psychologist with over 20 years' experience working with children, adolescents, and adults. Jill is a former Director of CampCare, a bereavement day camp for children and adolescents and worked as an Educational Therapist with emotionally disturbed children. At present, Jill maintains a private practice in Skokie, IL. When she is not working with her clients, she loves spending time with her family, taking pottery classes, gardening, walking her dog, and hunting for sea glass at the beach.

Both authors can be reached at *carryyourheart128@gmail.com*

For Carol, whose heart I forever carry in mine.

Contents

PREFACE

B efore we begin, let me offer a few disclaimers. This book was written primarily for men. Women have similar experiences, but also several characteristic differences in terms of processing grief, maintaining support groups and dealing with living alone. I received invaluable insights from talking to many widowed friends, but at the end of the day I cannot represent them with the same sort of "insider" knowledge that I have as a man. That being said, I believe women can benefit from many of the insights in this book.

The men quoted here from our men's group are generally older – our children are out of the house. While we love our children dearly and still want to address their emotional needs, we are largely free to concentrate on ourselves. Fathers with small children represent an entirely different dynamic, as the children become the focus of attention and the father's needs become secondary.

I recount many stories here. I was personally helped by hearing others tell their stories, and I believe these, in turn, will help you or someone you care about. There is nothing clinical about this, per se, but many do find it therapeutic. One of the first things you realize is that you're not alone, you're not abnormal. You just happened to have been dealt a terrible blow. Please note, however, that I am not a professional therapist and do not offer clinical advice. But many men who have lost their spouse after a long and loving marriage do seek professional counseling. When dealing with depression, anxiety, withdrawal and a wide range of emotions, it can be difficult to know just when one needs help. Consequently, I have invited Jill Schoeneman-Parker, a clinical psychologist, to offer a chapter on seeking professional advice. It's an important subject and I think you will find her comments relevant and informative.

Finally, everyone quoted in this book is a real person. I owe each of them immense gratitude for their honest, candid conversations, sharing with me, and now you, their inner-most feelings.

INTRODUCTION

It never hurts less; it just hurts less often.

Widow of victim of American Airlines
Flight 191 crash in Chicago

August 7, 2014 was our 43rd wedding anniversary. That's when I first noticed the limp.

Carol and I met in college in 1968. Quincy College, now Quincy University, a small Catholic college in southern Illinois, was the perfect place for young students to meet, although for us it surely wasn't love at first sight. In fact, we couldn't stand each other the first time we met, outside of the local bowling alley. But somehow, a year later we reconnected and never parted ways after that. I think it was on our third date that Carol told me that she wanted two boys, and she even had the names picked out, Stephen and Patrick.

We were almost the same age. She was not quite two months older, but she was a year ahead of me in school. Upon graduation with a degree in elementary education, she had just one job interview, Saints Faith, Hope and Charity Catholic School in Winnetka, Illinois, and it would be the only paying job she would ever have. Teaching was her mission in life and she embraced every day of it. She loved the children and they

1

loved her. We got engaged at Christmas of my senior year and were married right after my graduation. We never did have Stephen and Patrick. Instead, God blessed us with Kate and Meghan, two wonderful girls who owned us both. They now have beautiful families of their own.

Carol was never one to run to the doctor. It wasn't until I insisted that she agreed to go. That was October 14, 2014. She said she was not in pain, but that her leg just did not seem to support her weight. That was strange because she walked a lot. In fact, when we went on our "strolls" together, I had to work to keep up. Somehow, and I'll never figure out exactly how, our family doctor knew what was wrong as soon as she told her story. He immediately sent her to an oncologist for tests. She had stage four breast cancer that had metastasized to her spinal column, liver, and possibly her brain. The weakness in her leg was due to a large growth, one of a dozen, on her spine that was blocking nerve impulses to her leg. The diagnosis was immediate and bleak. On our second visit, after a round of tests, Carol asked if she would live long enough to see the birth of Meghan's first child, who was due in mid-December. The oncologists did what they could, but she passed away on December 15, just two months after her first visit to the doctor. She never saw her grandson, born just six days later.

It is impossible to describe the pain, the anguish, the feeling of utter helplessness I felt after Carol's death; nothing can compare to the loss of a spouse, especially after a long and successful marriage. You look forward to the many happy days to come, and then, Wham! She's gone. You've lost your partner; you've lost that intimate connection. In a large sense, your future has been stolen from you. People will try to comfort you with all sorts of clichés, like "It takes time," or "She'll always be with us." Have you heard the old sentimental standard, "Memories are so we can have roses in the winter?" I have – several times! All from well-meaning family, friends, relatives, and coworkers who have no real idea what you are going through; they simply feel obligated to say *something*.

No amount of platitudes is going to make you feel better. People somehow think you will "get over it" or "past it" or be able to "move on." It doesn't work that way. You don't get over it; you learn to live with it. If you've been through such a loss, you know. There is no *Big Aha* moment where everything suddenly becomes crystal clear and from which you leap to a new life. You can't just flip a switch.

Instead of an epiphany, if you are paying attention, you will find a steady stream of little revelations to help you deal with the unexpected turns in your life. These can be seemingly insignificant events in your daily routine – events that, when reflected upon, can help you get to know yourself a little better; help you recognize and clarify both the how and the why of your emotions. I call these little nuggets of life experience *Little Ohs (as opposed to the one Big Aha)*. They are positive affirmations that, when taken with your own intuition and self-awareness, can help you cope with your loss and daily life. Like, *Oh*, if I get into a routine, I feel much better and get more done. Or *Oh*, if I learn to cook, I am much more self-sufficient. When you have one of these moments, it triggers a reaction; it makes you stop and think more clearly about your situation and clarifies your options. *Oh*, this is why I feel this way. Note that these *Little Ohs* lead to positive experiences. They are not negative; otherwise, they would be *Little Uh Ohs*. Or perhaps *Oh Nos*! Unfortunately, yes, we've all had a few of those too.

It is interesting that we sometimes find it easier to be candid with others than with ourselves. Self-delusion, denial, and apathy are ready quicksand, not to mention isolation and social withdrawal. Alternatively, we often find it easier to talk with someone who has also lost a spouse – they understand, they get it. We don't have to act the role of the grief-stricken partner, but instead can freely express ourselves and be comfortable in doing so. Conversations with these fellow widowers are frequently in short sentences, almost a private language, because you don't have to say much to each other to convey your story. But language has another side as well. The ability to clearly articulate your feelings can be cathartic. Expressing your feelings in an organized, well-thought-out manner helps you to clarify your inner-most emotions.

I am fortunate to have a deeply loving support team. Men seem to not often have a great many really close friends, of either gender. Mine helped me cope with a wild ride of emotions, from sorrow to anger and back to self-pity. But I made it, somehow.

Two years after Carol's passing, a neighbor and fellow church member lost his wife to a long illness. I sensed Rodger could use some support and invited him out to dinner, pub grub in a local tavern. We talked for about two hours, on everything from sports to local news to our children. Our losses were in there somewhere, but we didn't dwell on them. It was a good "guy's talk." Yet, I knew we had more to delve into. Rodger had a lot bottled up inside of him, and I wanted to help him get it out. Interestingly, I had an inkling that this was helping me as well. I was as much a listener as I was in the telling of my own story. Rodger agreed to a second meeting and once the conversation restarted, there was no turning back. We even laughed. Actually, quite a bit. Equally important, we decided to invite a few other men of similar situation in the parish to join us.

With a core of five, including Jim, Ted, and Mark, and later a few newcomers, we started meeting for lunch the first Thursday of every month. The conversation is free-flowing and there is almost nothing out of bounds. While we seldom dwell on our losses, every lunch seems to yield at least one *Little Oh* to help us cope – certainly worth the price of a cobb salad and an Arnold Palmer, the standard fare. Over those many months, I started jotting down notes on some of the compelling gems of lunch-time wisdom. Those notes and my own experiences resulted in what you are reading now.

The objective of this book is two-fold. First, to let you know that no matter what you feel, or how strange you might think your emotions are, you are not alone. Your experience of loss is certainly unique, as unique as was the relationship between you and your spouse. The aftermath is something we more commonly share. Case in point, the guys seldom ever shock each other at our lunches. The degree of emotion and the focus changes a bit from person to person, but no one is surprised by anything anymore.

My second objective is to share some of the observations and lessons I've picked up along the way, those *Little Ohs*, many of which were uncovered in our group conversations. As mundane as they may seem, I found them immensely helpful as I began to navigate life after losing Carol. I hope you will, too.

I also hope this book encourages you to form your own groups. To be able to talk about your spouse, your loss, your children, and your future with other guys in the same boat can mean all the difference in the world. The price is some personal vulnerability, but the payoff is incalculable. If you have lost a spouse, it's my sincere desire that you find the same kind of peace and camaraderie as we did. You won't regret it.

THE ART OF TRIBAL THERAPY

◇◇◇◇◇◇◇◇◇◇◇◇◇◇◇◇◇◇◇◇◇◇◇◇◇◇◇◇◇◇◇◇◇◇◇◇◇◇◇

Under the shelter of each other, people survive.

OLD GAELIC SAYING

E veryone's life journey is different. I had 60 days before I lost Carol. At least I can be thankful she did not suffer long. A friend's wife suffered through ALS for four years. Every situation is unique and deeply personal, but you will invariably find something you can directly relate to in almost every story.

With that, let's get into what goes on at our group lunches.

Understand, this is not grief counseling, professional advice or a religious encounter. The doctor is not in. But what we found, five regular guys, some who started as complete strangers, was that simply getting together once a month and talking was great therapy. When we first met at a local restaurant, our collective angst was like a big bubble hovering over the table. No one wanted to dive in. So we nibbled around the edges, talking sports, weather, and politics. Finally, I decided to just plunge in. "Show of hands," I asked, "How many of you don't bother to close the bathroom door anymore?" It was like a pin prick in that bubble. A hearty laugh and you could feel the angst just fall away. From then on, it was all the little stories, experiences, the *Little Ohs* that five guys who just met could each relate to. On second thought, the doctor is in – he is each of us.

In subsequent lunches, we found great relief in just talking about our new lives, not the entire time, but throughout the course of pleasant conversation. Someone would bring up an experience, or ask a question (lots of questions about downsizing, getting the kids to take their personal belongings, and even dating). And the more we met, the more comfortable we became sharing our thoughts. What's more, we came to genuinely care about each other.

I can't forget the time we were comparing notes about cleaning house and having a monthly maid service. The guys were trading ideas about what types of service and how often to use them. I said I really like my service, waxing poetic about how it gave me great comfort to open the door to the smell of Pine Sol, knowing that everything would be clean and in its place. And as I'm saying this, I'm thinking, this sounds really weird! Should I be confessing that I'm a neat freak? But then, I looked across the table at Mark who was smiling. "For me its Murphy's Oil Soap! Brings back great memories."

We all had a good chuckle. So, we know we are not alone. No matter how deep the emotion or silly the comment, there is always at least one or two of us who can relate.

As time goes on, a friend or family member might say to you, "It's been a year, shouldn't you try to move on?" You never get over the loss. But by sharing experiences, our own *Little Ohs*, we came to better recognize ourselves and cope. Together we are broadening our perspectives on our individual situations. Sharing is learning. In our group, we unwittingly give comfort to each other.

How do you know if your group is making progress? Interestingly, it's not by the amount of time or the quality of the discussions about our wives and our grief. The two universal hallmarks of a good men's group are humor and one-upmanship. Let me explain.

Rodger was the breadwinner in his family, but his wife handled all of the finances. It's fair to say that Rodger was the ultimate hands-off guy. Shortly after his wife passed away, Rodger called the bank to have the credit cards switched to his name. The bank more or less said, "Not so fast." The credit cards were in her name and since she was deceased, those cards would be cancelled immediately. Rodger recounted with a great smile the first time he went to a gas station and had to pay cash inside. (I'm sure he wasn't smiling then.) Of course, we all enjoyed the story and shared a laugh with him. But I'm sure every one of us looked at our credit cards that night. If the group is going to be successful, you have to leave your ego at home.

I can't tell you how many stories started out, "This may sound weird, but…" The thing is that after a while, none of it sounds weird any more. That's because you are honest with yourself and your group. That's progress; that's healing.

One day someone introduced a new guy, John, into our group – everyone was welcome. Wanting to make him comfortable, I recounted the anecdote about closing the bathroom door. John's response was a robust, "I learned very early on in our marriage to at least put down the toilet seat!" We knew instantly he was a perfect fit!

The second most common phrase you will hear is, "Oh yeah, well I…" Mark was relating a story about visiting his daughter in Sydney, where he took a helicopter tour of the harbor and flew over the iconic Sydney Harbor Bridge. He had barely finished his story when Ted burst in with, "Oh yeah, well I *climbed* that bridge!" And then we all wanted to know the details.

Why are these two phenomena, weird stories and good-spirited one-upping each other, important? Because, believe it or not, they set the tone for deeper conversation. After the first two or three lunches, I suspect less than 10 percent of the time was spent on our life changes. Most of the time was spent on topics like sports, life, local news and upcoming travel. Those might not sound like earth-shattering topics, but you have to make those connections with each other before you can dive into the deeper topics with honesty and candor. And certainly, you don't want these lunches to turn into pity pools – you can do that all by yourself! You want to look forward to getting together with your group as a positive experience.

The safety of the community gives each of us the freedom and ability to express ourselves, to see, to learn, and some days, to just breathe.

THE WILD RIDE OF EMOTIONS

I have learned that while those who speak about one's miseries usually hurt, those who keep silence hurt more.

C.S. Lewis

Everyone deals with grief differently, just as we all deal with life differently. There is no single roadmap. The five of us each had a different approach that seemed to work in varying degrees. By talking about it, we each came to recognize the strengths and weaknesses of what we were doing. Then, by staying open to the possibilities, we allowed new approaches to emerge along the way.

The range of emotions and mood swings is incredible. If you haven't experienced such an intimate loss yourself, you might assume our days were filled with feelings of sadness. That's only part of the story. One of the most common emotions among the men I have spoken with was anger. I found this quite surprising, even though I had experienced a period of intense anger myself. Anger at God, anger at the doctors, even anger at Carol for leaving me. The intensity can be pretty strong; it can strike with little warning. (Again, while our tragedies are unique to each of us, the reactions are quite common.)

One day shortly after Carol died, I wanted to clean the dining room floor. I looked all over the house for the Swiffer. There are only so many places a Swiffer can hide. I became increasingly frustrated that I couldn't find it. I remember standing in the middle of the basement, looking up, and yelling, "Carol, where did you put the F-ing Swiffer!?" She didn't answer, but later I found it – in the F-ing closet!

I told this story to a friend who had lost his wife and was working with a grief counselor. As George tells it, at one point the counselor asked him if he had yelled yet. George was taken aback, mainly because he hadn't. The counselor wanted him to release some of that pent-up angst.

I learned that it's okay to be angry once in a while, as long as it does not become a habitual response.

Other times you find things your spouse did and you wonder, "What were they thinking?" Typically, for me, it's the small things. My wife was a marvel in the kitchen and was very organized. So why did I find at least ten bottles of spices way past their expiration dates? I mean years, not months! What was she thinking? But more importantly, how do we feel as we reflect back on incidents like this? Hopefully with fondness, even laughter, because that is part of what made her who she was.

I have a friend, Nance, who lost her husband of over 40 years to complications from heart surgery. Tim was one of my college roommates and he was a great guy. He had been ill and battling for quite some time. When he died, she was deeply hurt and missed him dearly. About a year later, she woke up one day and decided that her life was pretty good. She had a nice house, was financially secure, had lots of friends, and her golf game was picking up! She decided she was just going to be happy. But then a curious thing happened. Her newfound resolution was countered not by sadness, but by guilt, especially when she talked to widowed friends whose pain was still so evidently raw. Was her happiness a betrayal of her husband? Was it a sign that she no longer valued what they had had together? Talk to any counselor, and they will tell you these questions are quite natural. For Nance, it took a while to realize that if there was an illegitimate feeling, it was the guilt and not the happiness. Everyone works at their own pace and she decided she was not going to let a few people around her influence her newfound happiness.

It's not that Nance didn't miss her husband, but she was making a conscious decision to allow happiness back in. It's true: your new life won't ever be the same, but it doesn't have to be a perpetual dirge either. In the wild ride of emotions, you have to be a hero to yourself before you can be a good friend to others. One of those *Little Ohs*.

I didn't feel like a hero when I was Swiffering the dining room floor. But I did a few months later when I cleaned out the basement. I faced that ugly mess, and I conquered it! Sometimes being a hero in these little things makes all the difference!

Of course, birthdays, holidays, and special anniversaries can be especially troubling. It's good to share those days with family and friends. Many men noted that the second time around is often more difficult than the first. The first Christmas, for example, I found myself steeled against the emotions and the trauma – I just wanted to get through it. By the second year, I was less guarded. I wanted to experience some of the old joys of the season, which meant I felt Carol's absence more keenly. This was true for my children as well. Again, there is no one way to grieve. Just because your path isn't a straight line – and it never will be – doesn't mean you've lost your way.

Little fears, too, can take over. They may be reasonable, they may not. For me, it was an unreasonable fear of being locked out of my house. For the past 35 years I had never carried a house key, because someone was always home. And on the rare occasion when no one was home, there was always a spare in the garage. I addressed this by replacing the lock on the side door with a numeric keypad. Moral: resolve these little fears head on, and then move on.

The one thing all of us would tell you, and it needs no explanation: don't make decisions, especially big ones, when you are in a bad mood. Learn to take your own emotional inventory, and be patient with yourself. This self-awareness is not always easy, but it is one of the main things grief counselors work on with their patients – learning to recognize when you are in charge and when your emotions have taken control. Recognize the signs and don't let yourself become hijacked.

Conversely, we all experience little sentimental quirks. Several people have related how, even after many years, they only sleep on their side of the bed. I can relate to that.

For me, it was a watch Carol gave me for our 40th anniversary. It was expensive, so I reserved it for special occasions. Now, it is a lasting tangible reminder of her – so I still only wear it on special occasions. It's like I don't want to damage it through every day wear because it is special to her. You should revel in these little nuggets of sentiment, even chuckle. It's part of celebrating a life well-lived.

Full Disclosure: I also have a pair of fleece-lined slippers Carol gave me the year before she was diagnosed. They've been through a lot, including running out in the snow to get the newspaper, and they look it. But they keep my feet warm in a very special way. I'm sure you understand.

At one of our lunches, we noted how seemingly insignificant things would pop into our minds and cause us to think about our wives. Someone noted that a neighbor's house had been torn down and his first thought was that he had to tell his wife – even though she passed away three years ago. Then the conversation turned to how many times one of us would see something and instantly think, "Gee, I'm glad she's not around to see that!" Amazing, isn't it, how she has become such a big part of our subconscious. We sail in her wake where ever we go.

WITH FRIENDS LIKE THESE!

Never miss a good chance to shut up.

Will Rogers

Friends and family don't always know what to say. Often, coworkers don't either. Returning to work is like walking into a storm of well-intentioned but cringe-worthy comments. I just wanted to get past that first day and get back to a routine where I felt in charge of my life.

Part of healing is recognizing that other people may struggle with what to say. They may stumble, but they are well-meaning. This is true of family, and even your children. That first day at work I felt like the burden was on me to say something first, so that my co-workers would not have to. Then I got a bit angry: why was the burden on me? Eventually I realized the sooner I learned to accept that other people probably do not understand how my world has been completely rocked, the easier it is to not let awkward comments bother me.

I have often heard people recount how they avoided someone in the grocery store or after church because they knew that person would have something melodramatic to say. The worst are the ones who want to know all the details, as if sharing might help you cope. But instead

17

of sympathizing, they postulate alternative therapies you could have considered and recount how their second cousin in Poughkeepsie got gene therapy in Mexico! At times, you just don't have the patience. We've all been there, and there is no need to beat yourself up about it. It's one of those *Little Ohs* that once embraced makes your ability to cope with well-wishers a lot less stressful.

Your children will also be faced with an onslaught of comments. Their peers may try to be very open with them and say things like, "Gee, you must be terribly sad." While they are just trying to make a connection, comments like these are not comforting. You may want to have a conversation about social graces with your children so they can put things in perspective too.

Of course, there are still the grossly inappropriate encounters. One woman told of standing in the receiving line at her husband's wake when a man asked her if she had decided yet what she was going to do with his pick-up truck. My cousin Pat, whose husband Tony had been a real outdoorsman, shared that a few days after his funeral one of her husband's friends stopped by to offer more personal condolences. She said the visit ended with a hug at the front door, a peck on the cheek, and a reminder that he would be happy to "look over" his fishing tackle if she wanted.

Whether you are a man or a woman, you will undoubtedly come to the realization at some point that it is largely a couple's world. Now that you are single you may get fewer invitations from the old crowd. Over dinner one night, my friend Susan recounted how she was invited to a dinner party at an old friend's house and was excited at the prospect of seeing a lot of familiar faces. When she sat down for dinner, the host had left the chair opposite her empty, in remembrance of her husband. Susan was devastated – that was the last thing she wanted on that night. Perhaps at some point, remembering her husband might have been a good idea, but it's not something you just spring on someone unawares.

What is surprising is that once you start sharing these stories in a group, how many more come out. You just have to laugh and move on.

But wait a minute – let's not be too harsh. It's simply not an easy thing to comfort a grieving friend. What if the tables were turned? Well, in fact, they were. In a period of just over three months, I lost three friends. Two were neighbor men and one was a business associate. In all three instances, I found myself face to face with the widow, about to say many of the dumb things I decried in other people. Let's face it, it's hard to say the right thing, if there even is a "right" thing.

So, after examining my own attempts at condolence, I have come to several conclusions. The first is, keep it short. The more you say the more you risk getting into trouble. Someone in grief does not want to hear quotes from mystic poets or nifty sayings about God's plan.

Second, no one wants to hear words that minimize the situation, such as "At least we had her for all these years." or "At least his suffering is over." The loved one is gone and there is no upside. Don't try to find one just to have something to say.

Third, stick with the tried, true and simple. "I'm sorry for your loss," or "Your family is in my prayers."

Finally, if the opportunity presents itself for more conversation, come prepared with something positive to say about the deceased, especially something that will make the survivors feel good. "Tim was such an inspiration; he made a difference in my life." "Samantha always had a kind word for my mother. We will both remember her with love." "Bob gave me my first fly fishing lesson 20 years ago and even now, whenever I let one get away, I remember how he would yell at me." Yes, gentle humor, at the right time, is very loving.

TALK TO YOUR CHILDREN

The first duty of love is to listen.

PAUL TILLICH

H aving honest, candid conversations with your children is healthy, for both you and them. (Remember, the experience in our group was with older children, not youngsters.) It's okay for them to see you cry and to sense your pain. Just remember, they're used to seeing you strong, so this is new territory for them too. This is complicated for them because they have lost a mother, the family dynamic has been torpedoed and their father is suffering as well. They don't always know what to say. Essentially, they don't know where to put their sadness. They are hurting for them-selves and they are hurting for you, but probably less equipped than you to deal with the pain. Consequently, they may lash out in anger, redirect their anger toward others, or internalize their grief and clam up. And they might be fearful – what if something happens to you! But at the end of the day, most children want to know that you will survive, whatever that means, even if they don't know what they can do for you. Significantly, they will often take their cue from you and how you express your feelings to guide how to feel themselves.

Talking with my kids was quite an experience. After Carol died, I told my two daughters that the second half of my life would not necessarily be like the first half, as much as I love and miss their mom. Then I threatened to move to Alaska, just to keep them on their toes. Suddenly my hiking in Death Valley or solo hikes in the Colorado Rockies was easier for them to accept. What I learned was not to surprise them. Whether it's deciding to take a trip, tossing old furniture, or going out for an occasional dinner with a female friend, let them in early, even if you don't have all the details worked out. This isn't necessarily to get their approval or permission. If your kids are at all like mine, they will have had enough shock in their lives, and their desire to see you whole and happy again will override any misgivings or fear of change. You can be their pillar and still pursue your own life, even if it's quite different from the one you led before. But open communication is the key.

Several men noted that at times, they experienced a bit of a pause before they would say something to their children about their mom. Typically, it goes like this: it's a beautiful day at the beach and your grandchildren look like the vision of happiness in their little swim suits and sun hats digging in the sand. You look at their parents, your children, and want to say, "Mom would be so proud!" But you can't, because it might bring up sad memories of the loss. That's natural. But the unscientific conclusion of my friends is that after a while it's okay, even healthy, to bring Mom into the picture. It reinforces everything positive we remember about her. Share the love. Share the joy. Strengthen your memories.

At one of our lunches, we had a lively conversation about leaving written instructions for our children in the event of our own deaths. We all had done something, ranging from the deed to the burial plot to a list of passwords on all of our accounts. It was fun seeing who had considered what, and what else we had to think about. At the end of the meal we practically had a 'How-To seminar' for estate instructions. We did what we thought we had to do, and we thought we did a pretty good job. My outline of estate instructions is in the Appendix.

Then the real discussion started. How many of our children actually read what we had provided? The general consensus was that none of them had read it, or even skimmed through it. No matter how important these instructions are, they're the last things your children want to read after losing one of their parents. The idea of losing you too is almost incomprehensible. Keep this in mind when you talk to your kids. Their tightrope can be just as narrow and just as harrowing as your own.

And remember, sometimes the best conversation you can have with your son or daughter is you just listening to them. They're figuring things out as they go. They may have good, well-meaning friends they can talk to – but friends, as we know, will often want to jump to solutions without understanding what we're experiencing. A safe sounding board, someone who can give them space to process out loud, might be just what your kids need at the moment.

KEEPING BUSY

*Keeping busy and
making optimism a way of
life can restore
your faith in
yourself.*

Lucille Ball

Keeping a schedule, maintaining a routine is important. Get up at the same time every day. Go to bed at the same time – don't stay up late. Don't fritter away the day. I know, this sounds like cheap advice from your mother. But when you're in the throes of loss, gutted of all your normal routines and motivations, it's easy to fall into a slump.

At first, I slept late, frittered away the morning, had lunch and then did a few chores. One day, I am still not sure what motivated me, I decided to get up and go to 8:00 a.m. mass. I found the discipline of getting up every morning and getting dressed in something other than sweats was invigorating. Then I started planning the errands I could do right after mass. (Since I was already up and dressed.) It's amazing how many places, grocery stores, dry cleaners, and hardware stores, are open early.

I discovered that if I got my chores out of the way early, I had a sense of accomplishment. I did something other than lay around. Then I had a big chunk of time to exercise. I do a lot of walking, hiking, and biking. I can't over emphasize the benefits of fresh air and exercise. I even joined a kick boxing gym. Life is simply more enjoyable if you keep moving.

Don't misunderstand – I'm not saying you should keep yourself busy so you don't think about your spouse. I'm not prescribing a diversion tactic. I have met some men who have tried that, throwing themselves into some frantic pursuit as a way to cope, a way to drown their grief with constant motion and noise. I'm not talking about escape. I'm talking about a healthy, sustainable lifestyle that will help you do everything better, including remembering and honoring your beloved.

What really helped me turn the corner was to then develop a sense of purpose, and this is huge. My role had always been the provider. Now the kids are out of the house and I have lost my spouse. Who do I provide for? I looked around and decided to join the board of the Northeastern Illinois University Foundation. We serve Hispanic and minority students, many first-generation college students in their families. I didn't recognize it immediately, but I have come to fully embrace the idea of channeling my energy into something positive, something bigger than me. I feel good about myself. Of course, it is also rewarding to see these students succeed.

Read *Make Your Bed* by Admiral William McRaven (U.S. Navy Retired). It's an easy and enjoyable read. He talks about accomplishing something small first thing each morning to kick off the day, like making your bed. I endorse his view, and add that there is also great benefit to getting into a made bed at night. Going to bed should be a source of comfort, inviting even, not crawling into rumpled sheets to crash after another disappointing day, hoping that sleep will be some sort of refuge.

There's also a lot to be said for being organized. We've lived with structure and control our entire lives, starting with the morning bell in kindergarten. At this point in your life, with the kids out of the house and your wife in Heaven, there may not seem like much need for structure. It may even come as a shock, this new absence of direction. Kick back, so what! Pay those bills tomorrow! But without routine and structure, it is too easy to accumulate a host of small bad habits that can eventually grow into real trouble. The best way to project you new future is to reinvent it. Take charge!

A schedule puts you in control, both today and for the future. It's one of those *Little Ohs*.

Most important, don't forget your friends. They can be a great source of comfort and enjoyment without you even being aware. Besides the group I've been talking about, I also get together with a group of former finance and legal department associates from G. D. Searle, where I had worked for about 15 years. It has been over 35 years since we last worked together, but we've stayed in touch and get together a couple of times a year. In a sense, we have grown up together. We've raised children, welcomed grandchildren, and experienced life's ups and downs. Those friendships are life sustaining. Then there are the ROMEOs (Retired Old Men Eating Out) – an eclectic bunch of retirees who have lunch once a month just to chew the fat and swap lies.

Alone time can be important. But isolation is the enemy. Cultivating friendships, whether individually or through groups, is good for both the body and the soul. Research has shown a distinct correlation between friendship and improved cardiovascular functions, the immune system and even sleep patterns. We always knew socializing with a friend, even just a walk through the neighborhood or a cup of coffee in the morning, had an impact on our emotional well-being. But now we know so much more. So get out and socialize; don't turn down opportunities. People with robust friendships live longer too. It stirs the blood, the body and the mind. Yep, another *Little Oh*.

THE POWER OF FAITH

Hope is like the sun. If you only believe it when you can see it, you'll never get through the night.

LEIA ORGANA
STAR WARS: THE LAST JEDI

I have been very fortunate in my journey. Some days I actually surprise myself. I've had incredible highs and devastating lows. I've conducted myself very well at times, and as I look back, there were times I would not recognize who I was. I've witnessed the birth of two more grandchildren and watched all of them grow. I've missed my wife terribly, never more so than when within about a three-month period both of my daughters suffered miscarriages. What's a dad to say? Why us? Why me? Where's Carol when we really need her?

My lowest point was coming home from my first day back at work after Carol died. We lived in Winnetka, a suburb of Chicago. I took a commuter train into the city every day; the station was less than a mile from our house. It was mid-January, freezing cold, ice on the sidewalks, and not a ray of sunlight as I walked home that evening. It would be the first time in I don't know how many years that there would be no one to greet me, no dinner, no smiling face. Not even a light on. As I said, it was bitter cold, and my head kept telling me to step up the pace. My heart said to slow down. I didn't want to meet the inevitable any sooner than I had to. My heart won out, and I slowed my pace and pulled up my collar.

I am reminded of the famous Emanuel Leutze painting, *Washington Crossing the Delaware*. You've seen it a hundred times, even if you don't recognize the painter. There is George, in the front of the boat, looking steadfastly forward, mission clearly in mind, collar turned up, the weather be damned! We all need to be like George, but the gale forces buffeting our faces can be overwhelming. There were times I would have much preferred to be crouched down in the back of the boat – let someone else take the lead for me. George Washington had a great sense of self; he had mission and purpose. He knew his calling was something much bigger. Me, in the face of adversity, I sometimes just wanted to get through the day.

The one thing I have learned through all of this is that I can't do it alone. No one can. The question is, in your life, is God one of those persons you need?

That's a tough question for a lot of people. I am Catholic, but I would not describe myself as overly religious. I am certainly not very prayerful. I suppose that's a confession of sorts, but when I hear people talk about praying, it seems they are usually praying for something to happen: their son to get into college, to pass a test, or to have a good medical exam. Please dear God, let the Cubs win! If those are the sorts of prayers God answers, why did it take the Cubs a hundred years to get back to the World Series? I realize there are other ways to talk to God that are less mercenary, but when it comes to pleading for a particular outcome, I'm of the old school: God helps those who help themselves. I find more inner peace in praying for things like strength and guidance.

All the same, I found myself going to 8:00 am weekday mass more often. Yes, the discipline of getting up and getting dressed helped keep me on a schedule and my mornings became much more productive. But I gained a sense of calm too. I had a chance to reflect on things. And to hear some really great sermons. There was always a little takeaway. Is that faith? Is that prayer? I don't know.

(Why is it that the really great sermons are at 8:00 am during the week when only a few people are present and the Sunday sermon is about what sinners we are?)

When I talked to friends about writing this book, I shared the various chapters I planned to cover. Several of them chastised me for not including a chapter on faith. So, one day at our men's lunch, I came right out and asked what role faith played in their journey. Now at this point, we had been meeting for about a year and there was almost nothing we could not discuss. But when I posed the faith question, they all clammed up; everyone was uncomfortable. When I pressed, they all said faith played an important part in their lives, but could not be more specific than that.

My cousin lost her husband several years ago and she recently told me that the comfort provided to her through her church served to increase her faith. She said she felt a certain connection to God, a sense of His purpose. Mary had faith before her loss; many people don't. And if you don't have faith at the outset, you can't just convert when you need it.

I have come to a few conclusions. The first is that faith is deeply personal. So it is only natural that we have a difficult time explaining it. The one common thread is that it involves giving ourselves up to a higher authority.

Second, faith gives us a way to cope, a way to say to God, "Here, you take this burden. I am in Your hands."

Third, I suspect God does indeed answer a lot of prayers, but He doesn't always answer them in the way you were expecting. Be open to life all around you – His answer may already be right there in front of you.

What role religion plays in how you deal with loss is sure to be very personal to you. I do know that without faith there is no hope. And after all, isn't that what this is all about?

I have a friend who says, "It's good to have God in your pocket." Perhaps, with faith, it's even better to know that you're in God's pocket.

SUNNY SKIES AND OTHER PROBLEMS

<><><><><><><><><><><><><><><><><><><><><><><><><><><><>

*We don't
laugh because
we are happy,
we're happy
because we
laugh.*

WILLIAM JAMES

My grandfather Jacob Roskopf was a farmer from Hartington, a small town in rural northeast Nebraska. When I was a boy our family would go back there to visit relatives in the summer. One of my most vivid memories was a day spent fishing.

My dad, grandpa, an uncle and I had gone fishing for trout in a local stream. It was a beautiful, sunny day – clear sky and the fish were biting. For a small boy, it was quite an adventure. As I was sitting by the side of the stream a large crow flew overhead and, as crows often do, it pooped. Right on the side of my head – a big bird poop running down my right temple. I recoiled in horror, hands outstretched, not knowing if I should try to wipe it off, which might make it worse, or just stick my head in the stream. And the fact that my dad and uncle were laughing only made it worse. Grandpa, ever the pragmatic farmer, put it all in perspective when he looked at me with a knowing smile and calmly said, "You should be thankful cows don't fly!"

Years later, I have come to appreciate his wisdom. No matter how sunny our skies, how clear the stream, we are all going to have bird-shit days. We have to deal with them. Most important, it doesn't have to be hopeless.

After Carol died, I went through a brief period of alternating anger and self-doubt. Essentially, "Why me?" With all the schmucks in the world, what had I done to deserve this? It affected my outlook on almost everything. One summer day I had scheduled my car for routine mainte-nance – not an inexpensive affair for the latest wonder of German engi-neering. I woke up that morning with a sense of dread and, honestly, a tinge of anger. It was not going to be cheap; they would no doubt find other things that needed fixing, and they would keep the car for at least another day. That afternoon, I got the call that my car was ready. As Gunnar handed me the keys, he said with a smile that they also washed the car and filled up the windshield washer fluid. I was so shocked I blurted out, "What, and not the gas tank?" He retorted that they try not to put windshield washer in customers' gas tanks!

I laughed at myself as I drove out. Have you ever had that happen to you? You foresee a bird-shit event in your future and you get your hackles all good and raised for it, only to discover clear skies and no crows. It's almost disappointing. There's suddenly nowhere to vent, no target to rail against. I felt like I needed to put on boxing gloves or take an axe to a tree to release all that pent-up emotion. I told this story to my brother Jim and he responded with a chuckle, "You just don't want to be happy, do you?" I would never admit that he is right – I'm not that big a person! But he does have a point. You have to decide what you want. If you want to be happy, it has to be a big, strong commitment, not some wishy-washy desire that can easily be dumped on. If you're always looking for crows on your horizon, you'll eventually find them. In the meantime, you're missing the scenery. Aristotle said that courage is the first of human qualities because it is the quality that guarantees the others. A *Little Oh* I learned: it takes courage to be happy, courage to expect good things in the aftermath of a deep loss.

I also learned that if you nurse your worst fears, you can fall into a downward spiral, a vicious cycle. When things go right, you are surprised. The real danger is when they go wrong, because you then reinforce your expectation that everything is hopeless.

The trick is to recognize those bird-shit days and take them for what they are. A little perspective helps (thanks Grandpa). Achieving a level of contentment, acceptance of your feelings, can keep you on a more even keel.

I have asked Jill Schoeneman-Parker, Psy. D., a Licensed Clinical Psychologist, to clarify some of this for us. Sadness, anguish, even despair are all part of the grieving process. But they are just one part. It is when these feelings take over that you might need professional help. The following chapter contains great advice from someone who has seen a lot.

SEEKING PROFESSIONAL HELP

◇◇◇◇◇◇◇◇◇◇◇◇◇◇◇◇◇◇◇◇◇◇◇◇◇◇◇◇◇◇◇◇◇◇◇◇

My name is Jill Schoeneman-Parker and I am a Licensed Clinical Psychologist. I have been in practice for over 20 years. I have also worked for a hospice agency for a number of years, directing a bereavement camp for kids and teens. I met John a few years ago when we sat next to each other in a pottery class. We would on occasion chuckle about the "drama" in our class and in our own lives. I have two teenagers – I know all about drama! But drama is not the same as trauma.

We all experience difficult and painful moments in life. From the time we take our very first steps in life, we learn about falling down. With support and encouragement, we get back up and try again. Eventually we even learn to run. Life is, unfortunately, chock full of hurts. But hurt is different from trauma too. Trauma is created by an event which elevates the level of stress a person experiences and overwhelms one's inner resources. It taxes a person's ability to cope with that experience, and process the emotions involved with it. The extent of the trauma is impacted by several things, including the intensity of the event, how personal it is, and the complexity of the situation. It can be really complicated! So, let me see if I can simplify it a bit for you.

Let's start with a basic question: **Why do people seek grief counseling?** A simple question, but a million answers. Every one of us is different. Some have decided on their own that they want a little extra support. Some come because their family has urged them. Others because their doctor has told them they need to. Some come kicking and screaming, so to speak. Some come when the pain is too intense, creating difficulty navigating daily life; they feel immobilized. They may even feel hopeless about their future. Some come with only the desire to be heard and validated. And some come because they just don't know what else to do. Actually, many people are unable to express their reasons in concise terms. This is not surprising – their world is not as concrete as it used to be either.

There is no right or wrong reason for seeking counseling. There is no judgment. But I will share this with you: after coming for several sessions, a frequent comment is, "I didn't know how deep my grief was." That is very telling. Our self-mirror is not very clear – in fact, it can be quite deceptive. So, if you are not sure counseling is for you, I encourage you to try a few sessions. If you then decide it's not for you, simply move on. What have you got to lose?

The next question is: **Do I need grief counseling?** The short answer is, maybe. You may not be able to clearly see yourself; you don't always recognize why you feel the way you do. You just know that things are not clear. It's as if time is now divided into before and after.

Usually there is a range of emotions during the grieving process. Sometimes nothing feels right. There is no "normal" or going back to how things "used to be." There can be fluctuations throughout the course of a day. You might be feeling okay – until you're not. Maybe there is a lot of "foggy brain" happening or maybe you are "feeling nothing." Keep in mind, "feeling nothing" at times or "feeling numb" is a valid human emotion too. When you're processing a deep loss, the numbness or void is just as significant as anger or sadness or confusion or loneliness.

What if the sadness, loneliness, and other painful feelings linger? While these feelings are normal, grief counseling can help you manage them to an acceptable level. That in itself can be very therapeutic. I'll talk more about how that works in a minute. It's not the painful feelings that worry us therapists – we know you will have them – it's the potential complication of depression and giving up on living that is concerning. The effects of retreating from the world and focusing on one's own self-defeating emotions can spiral into something deeper – major depression.

Major Depressive Disorder, the clinical term, is not the same as feeling sad or down. In simple terms, depression includes a lengthy depressed mood, a loss of interest or pleasure in daily activities, and difficulty with sleeping, changes in eating, concentrating, lack of energy, or sense of not having a future. This is not a comprehensive list, but you get the idea. However, grief and depression can co-exist and sometimes grief can trigger a major depressive episode. The symptoms are similar, so a diagnosis with a trained therapist is important. Self-diagnosis is virtually impossible. The difference between grief and depression is that the sadness in grief looks more like waves that come and go, and they will be triggered by thoughts or reminders of your loved one. You might feel sad, but able to enjoy parts of your day too. This is typical of the grieving process. With depression, the sadness tends to be more persistent, pervasive and debilitating. There are a lot of the nuances to these complex feelings – lots of grey here. An example might help to illustrate the differences.

One woman, after the death of her husband, confided that she got up every morning, made her bed, ate a healthy breakfast, and tidied up the kitchen. Then she spent the rest of the day sitting and counting the hours until she could go back to bed. This had been going on for three months. This is not typical grief, this is depression. With grief, she might be sad, somedays a lot more than others, but she still would have been able to get dressed and go out for lunch with her friends, and share a few laughs.

Many people experience great relief through grief counseling. Even in the absence of depression, grief is a wild bunch of taxing emotions. Facing it head-on can be daunting. Many people derive benefit from initial weekly sessions and eventually taper off to something less frequent. Others simply like to have what they call their monthly "check in" just to keep tabs on their emotions and touch base with someone else who knows their story and struggle. I even have a client who comes in just to talk once a year on the anniversary of her son's death. It's always your decision.

The final question is: **What will I get out of grief counseling?**

I cringe when I hear people say something like "It's been a long time.... when will you get over it?" The short answer is, never. Coping with the loss of a spouse or a child or any loved one is a lifelong journey. We do not get "over it," we get "through it." My job is to help you see yourself, your emotions, and your environment more clearly so that you can have greater acceptance and ability to cope.

There are no simple solutions. On one hand, you can't ignore the pain; on the other, you can't just power through it. Similarly, no therapist has a magical book of "cures" either. Therapy is an interpersonal experience, meaning, we are discovering some things *together*, and while the therapist helps steer the boat, you get to decide where you want to go.

So, the first step is recognizing the depth of your grief. That sets the stage for the rest of your journey; you have to know where you are coming from in order to gauge where you want to go.

We do that, together, by peeling back the big onion of emotions, one layer at a time. Some people are more comfortable discussing their emotions than others. Many people don't recognize their emotions for what they are. In fact, a recent study found that the average person can only clearly identify three emotions at the time they experience them.

Sometimes all the different feelings blend into a big fog of "Why me?" A therapist can help you recognize and describe various emotions in more specific terms. A key part of the healing process is the ability to verbalize one's feelings – put actual names to how you feel. And that can be tough because, as much as we might want out of our current state, we don't want to describe ourselves as vulnerable, unable to cope, or needing to get "better," whatever that is. I constantly remind my clients that negative thoughts, self-doubt and intense sadness are normal. You've been through a lot, and I hope that with time you can accept these feelings as part of the journey. These are not failings. They are simply feelings to be acknowledged and processed. In order to deal with our overall condition, we have to be able to describe it somewhat concretely and acknowledge how we feel.

Identifying *triggers* is another step. A trigger is what evokes emotions, such as anger, anxiety and sadness. It may be an old photo, a song on the radio, a soft breeze on the evening patio. Interestingly, smells are one of the strongest triggers – the aroma of a favorite meal your spouse used to make on your birthday or the scent of fresh cut flowers. Seeing old handwritten notes or recipes can be powerful; they might even take your breath away. Not all triggers are negative, some things might prompt a happy memory. Through counseling you can learn to be more self-aware and understand your reactions. But know that this is not easy, as triggers connect you, today, with parts of your life that no longer exist the way they once did. When you decide to meet those feelings head-on, you are no longer engaged in avoidance, which only prolongs the pain.

I can't stress enough the importance of being able to clearly identify and verbalize your feelings. And it is important to do so without self-judgement. Negative feelings reinforce negative thinking and vice versa. Don't let yourself get stuck on that roller coaster. Through self-awareness you can monitor and even challenge yourself to "reframe" these unfortunate situations and keep on going. But sometimes we need a little extra help.

Up to now we have been talking about identifying your emotions. We also need to talk about your emotional state going forward – injecting some positivity into the equation. Having a plan that embraces tomorrow is important, and will help clarify the actions you need to take. Grieving is not a linear process; you don't go from A to B and eventually to Z and pronounce the journey over. Taking small steps, moving just a bit closer to where you want to be is a great approach to this journey.

Lastly, keep things simple. Find some joy when the sun finally comes out after endless days of grey skies. Take a walk. Surround yourself with nature. Keep a journal. Feel gratitude for having support from others. Create opportunities for your future (even if your heart isn't in it). Make plans to see a play, watch a sports event, watch a TV series, or try something new. This might all seem like a lot of work. It is. Adjusting is hard work. Growing is hard work.

Are there other options? Grief counseling typically is a very supportive and positive experience – but it does not have to be your only approach. Small, self-directed support groups can be quite helpful. If you are open to sharing your story and hearing those of other men and women in similar situations, you might be surprised. Expressing your feelings in these groups might help you to become a better listener as well as recognize your own emotions. Hearing the stories from others who walk the same walk reminds you that you are not alone. Keep in mind, a support group is not the same experience as counseling or group therapy. Some people have described their group meetings as light hearted and relaxed yet practical. I encourage you to explore your options and try different approaches to see what feels best for you.

Lastly, way back, as young children, when we began to learn how to take our first steps, we first stand, take a wobbly step, then stumble and fall. We feel hurt, then get back up. Maybe there was hesitation and maybe we needed reassurance. Fair to say, we all stood back up and tried again. We learned a very important life lesson – to keep going.

The loss of your spouse is one big tumble. You are standing back up, a step at a time. The lesson of our youth applies: keep going. There is life after the pain.

WHAT TO DO WITH ALL THIS STUFF

<><><><><><><><><><><><><><><><><><><><><><><><><><>

That's the whole meaning of life – trying
to find a place for all your stuff!

GEORGE CARLIN

When someone in our men's group discovers a good second-hand shop or charity thrift shop, especially one that picks up furniture, everyone immediately wants the details. Both men and women have commented that at some level they felt like they were abandoning their spouse if they got rid of their clothes and other possessions. And how to get rid of stuff can be just as difficult as deciding to do it in the first place.

What to do with your wife's clothes is often a dilemma and the cause of much grief. I wanted to donate Carol's clothes as quickly as possible – wanted a clean slate. Others in our group still had clothes in the closet years later. The problem is that no one wants most of it, even if it is in excellent condition. And at some level that hurts. You know what it is worth, you know that it is good, and you have an emotional attachment because you know how good she looked in it. But that's you. No one else sees that. It can be hard to accept that something that has personal, even intimate meaning to you has so little value to others. Part of the healing process is to get beyond that impasse. One way is to reinvest those things with new meaning. Find a favorite charity, a women's center for example, that you know your wife would be pleased to support. Make it a happy occasion. Reputable charities will certainly appreciate your donations.

My wife was an only child, so we, now I, inherited all of her parents' stuff too: china, stemware, silverware. What to do with it? Hard to toss, but the kids don't want it. I eventually donated most of it and gave some to her cousins. Frankly, it felt very liberating!

Divvying up some of your wife's possessions and deciding what to donate can also be a time of reminiscence with your children. It helps to share the joyful memories that a box of costume jewelry can bring, or even that ugly old sweater! But to just dive in to try to get it over with can be stressful, especially for the children. These things are memories for your family. You don't necessarily have to keep them, but you might want to allow some space for closure.

Your children may attach sentimental value to the things you least expect. Mine insisted I keep Carol's figure skates from high school, still in their original box, and a cowboy hat I bought for her on a trip to Dallas. There's seemingly no rhyme or reason to their choices, but arguing is pointless. Keep it, for their sake. After all, there's a lot of other stuff that really needs to go first.

The healing process for the entire family comes in many and varied forms. Take your time with these conversations – they are infinitely more precious than the actual decision on how to dispose of that sweater.

TO MOVE, OR NOT

◇◇

I hear there are people who actually enjoy moving.
Sounds like a disease to me – they must be unstable.

JAN NERUDA

A nother common topic at our lunches was when to move. The talk typically revolved around staying in the house, where it is familiar, comfortable and, if you're lucky, paid for. The hassle of moving looms large, even if you're downsizing. Then comes the angst of what to throw out. Avoidance can play a big part in these decisions. It took me almost four years to decide to move and I now regret not doing it sooner. It helped me get on with my life. Our house had become a museum of our past life – good for preserving memories, but not so good now. The question is: what makes sense for you today?

Your children may be sentimental at first – they've had so much change already. They may want to come back to the house, it's a place to center their lives. And they don't want you to get rid of certain things – anything from a favorite bowl to a painting. My daughter Meghan accused me of losing all sentimentality as I downsized and got rid of things. You might remind them, and yourself, that the love for your wife and the memories you created as a family all go with you. You'll carve out a space for them in your new surroundings, probably more than anyone could know. Memories, after all, are not in the things we carry, they're in our hearts, and perhaps live most vividly in the relationships we have with our children.

On the other hand, don't expect your kids to take a lot of things either – they want *you* to keep everything. They may have emotional attachments to certain things that you do not share. If those attachments are strong enough, they should take it. If not, remember, it is your life you are trying to keep focused.

I had a house sale, and an older woman came by to help me with the dishes and flatware. We ruminated about how hard it is to let go of things, even if they had not been used in years. After a bit, she looked me right in the eyes and said, "You know, we collect stuff all our lives and then, one day we wake up and realize our stuff owns us." Needless to say, it all went that day! Downsizing, simplifying, was one of the best things I ever did.

When cleaning house, start small, with daily or weekly achievable goals. One closet, one box, one dresser. You can't do it all at once, it will seem overwhelming. Gradually you will get into a rhythm and come to know the joy of feeling lighter!

I have a good friend, Phil, whom I have known for over 45 years. We worked together, played tennis together, and for a while even lived with our wives in the same apartment complex. We were close, but as our careers developed, I stayed in Chicago and Phil moved around the country. He finally ended up retiring in Tucson.

One day, I called Phil to tell him that I had sold the house and was moving to a condo, happy to have everything on one floor. Now I hadn't actually seen Phil in a few years, but we talked and a month or so later, I made the trip to Tucson for a long weekend visit.

At dinner the first night, he told me how he could tell from my voice on the phone that I was a lot happier. Now I hadn't actually seen the guy in at least five years, but somehow, he knew. And he was right. Was it because I was happier on that call, or that some sadness, or stress, or whatever had crept into my voice in previous calls?

Moving was very hard, especially cleaning out and disposing of 45 years of accumulated "stuff." But, like I said, it was one of the best things I could have done. And it's interesting how other people notice things that we don't notice in ourselves. Frankly, I thought I had been coping very well.

Whether it's moving or anything else, we all need a Phil. We all need that honest friend who can help us see through our own blind spots and adjust course as necessary, whether we decide to pack up or stay put.

DATING AND COMPANIONSHIP

<><><><><><><><><><><><><><><><><><><><><><><><>

*If you are not happy with yourself, you won't be happy
with someone else. In fact, you'll probably be miserable.*

D ating can be a touchy subject and everyone has their own perspective. Many in our group were not interested in actively dating, but said they might be open to something some time. After a while though, friends might want to fix you up. They think they know what you want – even when you're not sure yourself. A friend once tried to fix me up with a woman from church and it turned out she was only interested in finding someone who could drive at night!

No one wants to sound like a crusty old recluse, but I had several men comment that they did not want anyone impinging on their freedom, their time, or their personal space. And especially not their closets! That's always good for a laugh, but revealing too. We know that having a new relationship with someone means giving up a part of ourselves. If it was anything, marriage was a daily dance of give and take. For me, the rewards were worth it – infinitely so. But the fact remains: successful relationships are hard work.

Of course, you don't have to enter the dating scene looking only for a marriage partner; you don't have to put your closet in immediate danger. But you *do* have to be engaged in the other person, honest about what it is you are looking for, and ready to share yourself at some level beyond the merely superficial. If you're not willing to accept this bare minimum, you might not be ready to date quite yet. My advice? Whatever you choose, don't let fear, discomfort or the risk of getting rejected work against what you really want.

As it stands, you'll probably have enough complications to deal with. For those who have lost a spouse, dating can feel like a betrayal. Admittedly, I sometimes asked myself if it wasn't just outright guilt. Why would I want to find someone new when everyone knows how wonderful Carol was? This is especially close to the surface early on. It can pop up in conversations with your children about dating. Decide carefully what you want to share with them and when. You may feel a need to get out of the house and enjoy life again, but they might see things differently. Be prepared for their skepticism and accept it as an expression of their love for both you and their mother. My learning here was to recognize that moving *on* doesn't mean moving *past* your spouse; it simply means not getting stuck.

Your prior life is another curve you'll probably have to navigate. The ever-present legacy of your spouse can put a lot of pressure on a new relationship, even a casual one – sometimes more than it can bear. If your partner is thinking about how she can compete with your iconic memories, or you with hers, you're both in trouble. In my admittedly limited experience, the better path is to build on that legacy, not to try to replace it. The next person in your life can't compete with those memories, and it is similarly unwise for either of you to try to ignore them.

Personally, I had a wonderful experience that gave me a totally different, and very refreshing, perspective. I met Dawn at a local store where she worked. She recognized my name on the credit card and we realized that she had known Carol and we had a lot in common. We chatted a bit; she was very outgoing and cheerful and accepted my invitation to dinner. On a subsequent date, we were talking about Carol and at one point, thinking she might be uncomfortable with the conversation, I said to her, "We cannot let Carol be the elephant in the room." Her response was instantaneous and beautiful. She said, "She is not an elephant, she is not an impediment. We need to celebrate her life and keep her memory alive." I was floored...and grateful.

At one of our men's lunches, the talk turned to expectations in the new dating world. Mark made an interesting observation. With his wife, he never had to worry much about a filter on what he said. The intimacy they shared allowed them to communicate freely and they each "understood." Now, when he meets someone new, he has to consciously filter his comments. Furthermore, the standard has changed so much in recent years that "I don't even know what is acceptable anymore!" he said. A bunch of normally gregarious men suddenly turned quiet and returned to their salads.

But later, Jim took a different riff on Mark's observations. I don't know if he coined the phrase or not, but he called it the "intimacy of humor." Married people can communicate a lot through humor or gentle sarcasm. This is especially true when one party is making an unwelcomed point. "Well dear, I see Goodwill just announced they are no longer accepting triple-pleated trousers with frayed cuffs." It's that special way of communicating, endearing actually. But be careful using this tactic with your new date! Without a history, it can easily backfire.

I mentioned talking to your children about dating. That's always interesting! They will be naturally protective of you. And while they may begrudgingly accept that you're getting back out, they'll likely have their own images of what your dating partner should be like. I once met a woman while hiking in Death Valley with my brother Bill. Since it was the desert, I'll call her Sandy. I currently live just outside Chicago and she lived in St. Louis, where I grew up. We had a nice conversation, but then went our separate ways in the parking lot. I commented to Bill that she was really nice; he poked me on the shoulder and insisted I run over and ask to meet her again. I just barely made it to her car as she was pulling out. We arranged that I would come down sometime, do a few touristy things and have dinner. At that point I had a phone number and that's all I knew about her – I had no idea what I would do when I got there.

Then I told my daughter. "How do you know she's not a serial killer?" she asked – this mysterious *someone* I met out in the middle of nowhere. When I later told Sandy about the conversation at dinner, she said she had the same reaction from her daughter!

Air Force Major (Ret.) Dan Rooney is quite a compelling individual. His book, *A Patriot's Calling*, is included in the 'Recommended Reading' at the end of this book. One of Dan's favorite sayings is, "Sometimes you have to go before you are ready." What he means is that you can't just sit around and wait for the perfect opportunity. You have to get off your duff and get started. That is never truer than with dating.

In the case of Sandy, boy oh boy, I was so far from ready! She was probably the first person I asked out, a little over two years after Carol died. Drop dead gorgeous and a great perspective on life. I was unprepared and the romance, if you could call it that, quickly fizzled. But I had a good time and I learned a little about myself and what it takes to have a successful date. We didn't talk again for two years. Interesting though, I value her insights. In fact, she is one of the people I asked to read the manuscript for this book. I didn't find what I was looking for in Death Valley, but maybe I got something better. Life is good. That's another

Little Oh and ultimately, I have to thank my brother for prodding me into learning it.

When Carol and I got married, marriage was one man, one woman, one house, one checking account. And when we could afford it, one car. Relationships don't have to be traditional – it all depends on whom you meet and their perspectives too.

My old boss Don shared with me that after his wife's death he met a local woman and they have a loving relationship. They spend time together, travel, and care deeply about each other. But neither of them is interested in marriage or the long-term obligations that come with it. They each have downsized homes near each other and "don't relish the idea of smashing our stuff together just to live together." Discussions about traveling, living arrangements, sharing expenses, financial independence, and leaving an estate for your children are all very important. These topics should be a way to get to know and understand your partner better, not a source of friction.

The next person in your life doesn't have to be that perfect match, she could just be a friend. Companionship isn't so bad, after all. In the meantime, it's best to focus on taking care of yourself, physically and emotionally. Keep that good balance and be open to the possibilities. Good things will happen – just be patient. It's another of those *Little Ohs.*

LESSONS IN POTTERY

*Concentrate on how far you've come, rather
than how far you have to go.*

UNKNOWN

One day while out grocery shopping, I happened upon a pottery shop, called, appropriately, *The Pot Shop*. I wandered in and the owner, a nice enough guy named Dominic, showed me around and explained how I could join a class for beginners. He seemed knowledgeable and invested in his craft, and I signed up on the spot.

It only took a couple of sessions to learn that the affable Dominic was an ex-Marine, Vietnam Purple Heart Veteran. Failure to clean up one's wheel and work area would result in a serious dressing down. Not following his instructions often resulted in very direct and sarcastic comments. The instructional sessions were great, but the accompanying chatter is what really made the class.

One of Dominic's favorite sayings is, "There is no crying in pottery." His point was that you can't get emotionally attached to a piece you are working on. If it fails, for any reason, you just scrape the clay off the wheel and start over. No big deal. Don't beat yourself up over it. What he didn't say, but you eventually learn for yourself, is that you get better not in spite of your mistakes, but because of them. Once you are tuned in, you realize that pottery is a continuous learning process. You master the wheel in large part by recognizing what went wrong and adapting better techniques. Sound familiar?

Unfortunately, in life there is crying. But with patience, self-awareness and a little tinkering, we can turn those lumps of clay into something nice. Which brings me to another lesson in pottery, called Kintsugi.

Kintsugi is the Japanese art of ceramic repair. You've probably seen it but did not know the technique or its storied background. Kintsugi literally translates into "golden joinery." Picture a small ceramic bowl, perfect in shape and size. Then one day it falls off the shelf and cracks into several pieces. But that's not the end of its value; it's not consigned to the scrap heap. A Kintsugi master will rejoin the pieces using a mixture of resin and gold powder. Whereas previously there might have been ugly repair cracks there are now rivulets of bright gold, craftsmanship worthy of admiration.

Western civilization is so focused on attaining perfection on the first go 'round that we cannot countenance anything less. Rather than embrace our wounds after the loss of our spouse, we internalize the pain and, at its extreme, see ourselves as less than ideal. We are somehow flawed, failed or future-less. The Japanese craftsman recognizes that the cracks are not the end of the piece. By embracing the flaws, he creates the beginning of a new and artful bowl. It is not easy work; it takes time and patience. But in the end, we celebrate the beauty of the restored piece, while fully acknowledging the cracks.

My pottery-mate Jill, who introduced me to Kintsugi, summed it up brilliantly and her observation has become my favorite *Little Oh*. "You have suffered a traumatic loss. You feel hurt, you feel broken. You have several jagged edges. But that doesn't mean you can't be beautiful again."

On December 15, 2014, part of me died with Carol. But a part of her remains living in me. I hold on to it, not just as a memory, but as a promise. I leave you with the words of poet E. E. Cummings. My daughter Kate shared his poem with me as we talked about this book and about our beloved wife and mother. The opening lines of this wonderful poem are:

I carry your heart with me
(I carry it in my heart)
I am never without it

Her memories are the gold that smooth my rough edges.

LIFE IS WORTH LIVING

Only that day dawns to which we are awake.

HENRY DAVID THOREAU

William James, the father of American psychology, published his seminal book, *Principles of Psychology*, in 1890. James was well ahead of his time in identifying the links between outlook, mental well-being and physical health. He said we have to go through the motions of being happy in order to actually be happy. We are happy because we smile, not the other way around. Over 130 years later, we call it "Fake it till you make it." I know, that is a gross generalization of his insights, but I have decided I am the king of faking it.

I am blessed with a great family, two brothers and a sister, supportive daughters, and a healthy social network. I decided early on that I had to be out of the house, outdoors if possible, and busy. I went hiking with my brother Bill: Sedona, Big Bend, Death Valley. Hiking and fly fishing in Colorado. I enrolled in pottery class so I could beat up a few pounds of clay. Bought a new bike. Volunteered at a local college. Joined a kick boxing club and kicked the heavy bag so hard and so often that I'd wake up at night with shooting pains in my butt. (That alone tells you that perhaps I should have sought professional help!)

I also had my group of fellow widowers: Mark, Jim, Rodger, Don, John, Ted and Mark. They made brief appearances throughout this book and they are all real people, in every sense of the phrase. In the strongest terms possible, I urge you to form your own group. You'll never regret it.

That triumvirate – mental health, physical wellness, and outlook – is a real difference maker. It took me a while to realize it, but when I did, it made a huge difference in my life. Cultivating good habits, like getting up, putting on clean clothes, and doing errands or going to mass gave me a sense of both purpose and accomplishment. You'd be surprised how many days a man can wear the same pair of jeans, not shave, not make the bed, and think nothing of it. Those bills, I can pay them tomorrow. I look back at the weeks and months after the funeral and I don't recognize myself. Yes, everyone goes through that wild ride of emotions, it is a natural part of a traumatic loss. But if I had let those corrosive self-doubts sabotage my outlook, I would never have made it. Progress is in degrees and, after five years, I still have a way to go. We don't ever get *over* it, we get *through* it. And frequently it is the little things that can either stifle your chances or open a new perspective. One *Little Oh* for me was in a light bulb.

I used to fanatically turn out the lights whenever I left a room – don't want to waste electricity! I didn't need much light anyway; it was just me. One cold winter evening I happened to notice how everything seemed just a bit cheerier when the house was lit up. As silly as it seems, it was a transcendent moment. That's when I got it – the mental health, physical wellness, outlook connection. That's when it all came together. I started faking it that night, when I decided not to be afraid of the light.

I don't fake it anymore – I don't need to. Sure, I still have my moments, drifting off to "Why World." But I don't have to force myself to get up in the morning anymore. Fortunately, my new bedroom windows face south and there are glorious rays of sunshine in the morning that won't be ignored. I have learned to let the positivity percolate up through everything I do. And if you really heed William James' advice, it's not at all faking it; it's taking charge of your life by being self-aware and changing your outlook. My fellow intrepid travelers know this, the road isn't easy. It takes courage and a big dollop of humor. So...

Throw open the curtains, turn on the lights,
Grow in your journey,
And when in doubt, just take the next step.

God bless you.

A PERSONAL POST SCRIPT: THRIVAL SKILLS

◇◇

S o, the book is finished. My intent was to share some of my stories and remind you that you are not alone in this journey. Although your experience is unique to you, the range of emotions and the hurdles you face are common to many of us. I also want to encourage you to form your own informal groups, share lunch or a drink, and engage in some tribal therapy, as I did with my men's group. I hope I have done that.

But as I look back at my notes in preparing for this book, it seems I may have stumbled upon some bigger life issues; issues I had not come to completely own up to. A lot of this book is about survival. Practical tips, the eat well, exercise, bathe regularly, and clip your toenails kind of stuff. But beyond survival skills there are thrival skills – what you need to do to thrive. Not only after a loss, but in life in general.

I'm not a psychologist – I have an MBA. Unfortunately, you can't analyze emotions on a spreadsheet. I didn't do much research beyond our men's group and talking to friends. I intentionally chose to avoid most current psychology literature because I didn't want it to influence my deeply personal thinking about death, loss and life thereafter. Coopting other people's theories might dampen my own thoughts. Nonetheless, I did, as I say, stumble on a few truths, at least true to me, which I would like to share with you. With that, here are my top five lessons learned.

Hope is not a virtue. Hope is a choice. It is a strong, deliberate, conscious choice. It is the recognition that things can be better, and that you are the only one who can make them so. That recognition, in turn, comes from introspection. The heart of meaningful introspection is vulnerability. And the only way to get to that vulnerability is to be brutally honest with yourself, and that takes courage.

So, progress, or healing, ultimately thriving, is a three-legged stool of hope, vulnerability and courage. It takes all three. And what are these three legs holding up, you ask? Action. You will never progress, you will never thrive, if you don't take action. You have to initiate the change you need. As the old saying goes, even if you are on the right track, you can still get run over if you aren't moving.

Is it hard? Hell yes! Is it worth it? That's the wrong question. The better question is, what's the alternative? Even now as I write these words, I find myself asking, did I really change, or am I still faking it? The answer in part, for me, is that this is not a *Big Aha* moment that changes life forever. It is a journey, and one that needs plenty of rest stops along the way. But I need to be clear about one point on faking it. Remember the quote from Major Dan Rooney, "Sometimes you have to go before you are ready." Faking it is not so much a false path, but one step along the path of real change. Just keep moving!

I define vulnerability as being open, honest, candid, to freely share your feelings, both with yourself and with others. It includes the risk that what you receive in return might not be what you were hoping for. The problem is, vulnerability is counter-intuitive. At the time when you most need to be strong, to steel yourself against whatever is out there, you do not want to be exposed as something less than what you are projecting of yourself. It is exactly at that point when you need to be vulnerable. That is the point when real progress is achieved. Which is why courage is such an important part of the stool.

Live deliberately. Don't march in other people's parade, your own is lively enough. Don't accept advice from others carte blanche. Stoked with your new vulnerability and courage, allow yourself to sit in the moment and think for yourself. First, it's okay to grieve. It's acceptable to be sad. The issue isn't the emotions, it's how we react to them. Eventually you will come to realize the grief does not have to consume you. Remember, give yourself permission to grieve honestly and allow yourself time.

Routine is good. Structure, especially in precarious times, helps keep our bearings. I advocated for setting a routine and accomplishing various tasks earlier in this book. But what I learned, the hard way, is that routine is not a panacea. In the early stages of grief, routine is a comfort, a welcome relief. But as time goes by it can be deceptive by distracting you from facing life head-on. Surprisingly, you can get comfortable in a routine and come to accept your grief. Comfort with grief? Doesn't sound right, does it? But it can happen. If you don't have hope, vulnerability and courage, you might find yourself sliding into some serious quicksand. The rhythm of routine deceives us. I read somewhere that salvation is disruptive. How true. You can, and should, create a new routine, but live it deliberately.

I also advocated for maintaining friendships and forming what I labeled tribal therapy groups. Once again, great ideas. But I found that being intentional is important. The best take-aways from these groups are ideas for success, lessons learned, ways to inject positivity into your life. The risk is that your friends, who think they know what you need, will lapse into serving only comfort food. You don't need to hear how sad it is, or that you'll have his or her memories, or now you can spend more time with the grandchildren. I suggest developing a good comfort food detector so you can sift out the warm but ultimately empty calories. What you need are ways to grow. Deliberately!

Change your narrative. All our lives we have been subconsciously constructing our life narrative. It is a story we tell ourselves about who we are, how we relate to others, our position in life, what has meaning to us. Our narrative gives us comfort by reassuring us of our worth. Then your spouse dies – the trauma and loss totally disrupt your narrative.

The challenge then is to build something new. The problem is that most of us strive for perfection and we refuse to accept anything less. And of course, we are all about comparisons to others. But our old life, pre-loss, was not always perfect either. We remember all the good things, rightfully so, and we ignore the imperfections we tolerated in the past. Consequently, we end up striving for the unattainable.

According to some researchers, the average person has upwards of 30,000 thoughts a day. And what do those thoughts have in common? First, by one estimate, 70 percent of those thoughts are negative. Second, most of those thoughts are the same ones we had the day before. Is it any wonder that it can be so hard to cope with loss? So, if you are going to succeed, you have to change your narrative. You have to build something new – possibly including a new life, new meaning, new goals. Start with a healthy reexamination of what is truly meaningful to you and consciously reinforce it.

Look for the Gooder Thing. I learned something from Carol when we were in college, and to honor that, I want to share it here. Every night, Carol would reflect on the events of the day and internally celebrate something positive or enjoyable that happened. She called it the 'Gooder Thing.' It could be a anything: a compliment from a professor, running into an old friend, the sight of a child screaming with delight on a swing. They were positive reaffirmations of a joyous life based on seemingly insignificant events in the hustle and bustle of everyday life.

I resurrected that practice about a year after she died. Many days, the Gooder Things were external, like a beautiful sunset or, once finding $5 in an old pair of sweatpants. But gradually the Gooder Things became more internal, more personal: how I felt, doing something for someone, having a laugh, completing a difficult task. Once I was thankful for having the control not to eat a second piece of cake! Any day when you can spend 30 seconds before going to bed, sifting through all the positive things that happened, and designating just one of them as that day's Gooder Thing, is a great day.

Do yourself a favor. You've come a long way, so be proud of yourself. Even if you feel like you have a ways to go, (and we all have those feelings), take comfort in all of the small steps. You can be brutally honest with yourself, and you need to be, but that doesn't mean you have to beat yourself up. That's a game you'll never win. Honesty and self-flagellation are two entirely different things!

Forget the comparisons – there is no winning in that. Everyone copes differently and external manifestations are not necessarily accurate reflections of how someone is doing internally. Your job is you, and only you.

Above all, no second guessing. Just like trekking through the wilderness, not every step is forward – circuitous routes often serve us well. I do a lot of hiking and I also know you have to take time to breathe and enjoy the scenery. We'll all get there at our own pace.

ACKNOWLEDGEMENTS

◇◇◇◇◇◇◇◇◇◇◇◇◇◇◇◇◇◇◇◇◇◇◇◇◇◇◇◇◇◇◇◇◇◇◇◇◇◇

First and foremost, I have to thank my two daughters, Kate and Meghan, for their support. I could not have done this without their love and encouragement.

Thanks to Jill Schoeneman-Parker for her guidance. Her chapter on seeking professional advice was great on its own. She also provided invaluable insights and clarity as I developed the initial manuscript.

Dave Bonick is the best editor I could have ever had. He appreciated my style and had the patience to walk me through the editing process. Together we killed several of my angels!

Special thanks to all my friends quoted in this book, especially our men's lunch group. You opened your hearts with stories, insights and guidance. Above all, you listened, which inspired me to take on this project.

Finally, I express my gratitude to two pairs of Merrell hiking boots and four pairs of Brooks running shoes, who valiantly gave up their soles, from the Colorado Rockies to Death Valley, on suburban streets and numerous trails and national parks, pounding out my frustrations and building a new future. And of course, thanks to my youngest brother

Bill, who accompanied me on many hikes, just to be sure the old man made it back.

APPENDIX

RECOMMENDED READING

These are some of the readings that I found helpful and inspiring.

Make Your Bed: Little Things That Can Change Your Life...And Maybe the World
By Admiral William H. McRaven (Retired)

A retired Navy SEAL provides words of encouragement to help you live up to your potential, even under the most difficult circumstances.

A Patriot's Calling: Life Between Fear and Faith
By Major Dan Rooney (Retired)

An Air Force F-16 fighter pilot and PGA pro relates how he, and you too, can make a difference by being prepared and mentally tough.

Desiderata
By Max Ehrmann

A beautiful poem about faith and self-affirmation.

i carry your heart with me (i carry it in my heart)
By E. E. Cummings

A touching poem of love.

ESTATE INSTRUCTIONS CHECKLIST

◇◇◇◇◇◇◇◇◇◇◇◇◇◇◇◇◇◇◇◇◇◇◇◇◇◇◇◇◇◇◇◇◇◇◇◇◇◇◇

Will
- Where is it?
- Summary
- Who are executors?
- Recommended attorney to contact if there are probate issues

Revocable/Irrevocable Trust
- Where is it?
- Summary
- Recommended attorney to contact if there are probate issues

Power of Attorney for Healthcare
- Where is it?
- Summary; who makes the decisions
- Recommended attorney to contact if there are any issues
- Do Not Resuscitate (DNR) instructions

Attorneys
- Advice/recommendations on attorneys to use
- Alternatives – Trusted family members for guidance

Other Documents
- Homeowners' insurance, auto insurance, auto lease/title/lien release, mortgage/deed, lease, etc.
- Where are they?
- Contact information

Other Assets
- Rental property, timeshares, second home, partnerships, etc.
- Documents
- Special instructions

Disposition of Other Assets
- Property not specifically enumerated in the will, e.g. who gets the antique clock.

Safe Deposit Box
- Who is authorized to have access?
- Are bank records current; children's correct married names?
- Where are the keys?
- What is in it?

Note: Many of the documents cited in this outline will likely be kept in the safe deposit box. It is recommended that all documents in the safe deposit box also be listed here as a way to double check that you have included everything, e.g. deed to the house, plot plan, jewelry, family documents, etc.

Checking Accounts
- Who is authorized to write checks against your checking/savings accounts?
- Access to online banking and paper checks
- Automatic payments, e.g. loans, utilities, credit cards
- Bank credit cards

Investment Accounts
- IRA/401(k)
- Health Savings Account
- Other accounts
- Details and account numbers
- Copies of Transfer on Death and/or Beneficiary forms
- Contact information

Automatic Transfers
- Details on any automatic transfers, e.g. monthly transfer from an investment account to a checking account for routine living expenses and automatic bill payments.

Life Insurance
- What policies do you have?
- Any coverage through current or previous employers?
- Where are the policies?
- Documentation on employer plans
- Who are beneficiaries?

Health Insurance
- Traditional health insurance
- Medicare
- Medicare Supplement Policies
- Provide details and contact information
- Remind heirs to contact Medicare and supplement insurance companies so they do not continue to bill you.

Social Security

- Where is the monthly benefit deposited?
- Remind heirs to contact SSA to stop benefit payments

Pension Plans
- Where is the monthly benefit deposited?
- Where is the documentation?
- Remind heirs to contact plan administrator to stop benefit payments
- Provide contact information

Employer
- Contact information
- Life insurance
- Health insurance
- Retirement plans

Home Safe/Gun Cabinet
- Keys or combination

Tax Returns

- Who helps prepare them?
- Contact information
- Where are prior returns?

Passwords
- Create a list of all IDs, passwords and security questions. Include everything: bank accounts, credit cards, social media accounts, frequent flier programs, hotel programs, computer access, Internet provider, health insurance accounts, Social Security account, etc.

Note: Do not keep the password list with this document, as it may be updated periodically. Keep the list in a secure file and simply let heirs know how to locate it.

Cemetery Plot
- Deed
- Headstone information
- Any instructions

Final Instructions
- Funeral arrangements/preferences
- Memorial services
- Obituary
- Charity/Donation wishes

Doctors
- Depending on individual circumstances, you may want to list all healthcare providers and contact information.

Note: Redundancy in this document is intentional. Your heirs will likely not be as focused as they might otherwise be when reading this. So, for example, keeping lawyers' names with the relevant documents and also developing a list of recommended attorneys by specialty makes sure they get to where they need to be.

◇◇◇◇◇◇◇◇◇